AIN'T MISBEHAVIN'

Words by
ANDY RAZAF

Music by
THOMAS "FATS" WALLER and HARRY BROOKS

Ain't Misbehavin' - 3 - 1

ALL MY TOMORROWS

Lyric by
SAMMY CAHN

Music by
JAMES VAN HEUSEN

14

But with you there at my side,— I'll soon be turn-ing the tide,— just

wait! As true, And All My Bright To-mor-rows be-

long to you!_____

Coda

All My Tomorrows - 3 - 3

ALL THE THINGS YOU ARE

Words by
OSCAR HAMMERSTEIN II
Moderately Slowly

Music by
JEROME KERN

You are the prom-ised kiss of spring-time That

makes the lone-ly win-ter seem long.

You are the breath-less hush of eve-ning That

All the Things You Are - 3 - 1

16

The lyrics under the music:

trem - bles on the brink of a love - ly song.

You are the an - gel glow that light a

star, The dear - est things I know

are what you are.

Chords: Abmaj9, Am7b5, D7, Gmaj7, Am7, D9, Gmaj7, G6, F#m7b5, B7b9, Emaj9, C7b9, C7

Tacet markings.

Footer: All the Things You Are - 3 - 2


ALONE TOGETHER

Words by
HOWARD DIETZ

Music by
ARTHUR SCHWARTZ

Alone Together - 4 - 1

Alone Together - 4 - 2

AS TIME GOES BY

Words and Music by
HERMAN HUPFELD

As Time Goes By - 2 - 1

AUTUMN IN NEW YORK

Words and Music by
VERNON DUKE

Autumn in New York - 4 - 1

AZURE

By
Duke Ellington and Irving Mills

Azure - 2 - 1

BILL BAILEY, WON'T YOU PLEASE COME HOME

Words and Music by
HUGHIE CANNON

Bill Bailey, Won't You Please Come Home - 2 - 1

THE BIRTH OF THE BLUES

Words by B.G. DeSYLVA and LEW BROWN
Music by RAY HENDERSON

The Birth of the Blues - 3 - 1

34

BLUESETTE

Words by
NORMAN GIMBEL

Music by
JEAN THIELEMANS

Moderate Waltz

G F#m7-5 B7-9

Poor lit - tle, sad lit - tle blue Blues - ette.
Long as there's love in your heart to share,

Em7 A7-9 Dm7 G7

Don't you cry, don't you fret.
dear Blues - ette, don't you des - pair.

Bluesette - 7 - 1

36

Bluesette - 7 - 2

38

BLUE MOON

Lyrics by
LORENZ HART

Music by
RICHARD RODGERS

Blue Moon - 2 - 1

BLUE RONDO A LA TURK

By
DAVE BRUBECK

46

Blue Rondo a La Turk - 10 - 4

Blue Rondo a La Turk - 10 - 6

1st Improvisation

2nd Improvisation

52

BODY AND SOUL

Words by
EDWARD HEYMAN, ROBERT SOUR
and FRANK EYTON

Music by
JOHN GREEN

Moderately, smoothly

BOY MEETS HORN

Words and Music by
DUKE ELLINGTON, IRVING MILLS
and REX STEWART

THE BOULEVARD OF BROKEN DREAMS

Words by
AL DUBIN

Music by
HARRY WARREN

The Boulevard of Broken Dreams - 5 - 1

BYE BYE BLACKBIRD

Words by
MORT DIXON

Music by
RAY HENDERSON

Bye Bye Blackbird - 3 - 1

where there's sun - shine ga - lore._____
now my dreams_____ will come true._____

Chorus:

Pack up all my care and woe, here I go sing - ing low,

bye bye black - bird._____

Where some - bod - y waits for me, sug - ar's sweet, so is she,

CARAVAN

By
DUKE ELLINGTON, IRVING MILLS
and JUAN TIZOL

Caravan - 4 - 1

68

COME BACK TO ME

Lyrics by
ALAN JAY LERNER

Music by
BURTON LANE

Refrain *(lively with intensity)*

1. Hear my voice where you are! Take a
2. (Blast your) hide, hear me call! Must I

train; Steal a car; Hop a freight; Grab a
fight cit - y hall? Here and now, damn it

Come Back to Me - 5 - 1

72

74

Come Back to Me - 5 - 5

CUTE

Words by
STANLEY STYNE

Music by
NEAL HEFTI

*May be sung as solo or duet

Cute - 3 - 1

DAYS OF WINE AND ROSES

Lyric by
JOHNNY MERCER

Music by
HENRY MANCINI

Days of Wine and Roses - 2 - 1

DESAFINADO
(Slightly Out of Tune)

Original Text by NEWTON MENDONCA
English Lyric by JON HENDRICKS and JESIE CAVANAUGH

Music by ANTONIO CARLOS JOBIM

Desafinado - 5 - 1

83

Desafinado - 5 - 4

84

Desafinado - 5 - 5

DO NOTHIN' TILL YOU HEAR FROM ME

Lyric by
BOB RUSSELL

Music by
DUKE ELLINGTON

86

Do Nothin' Till You Hear From Me - 3 - 3

DON'T BLAME ME

Lyric by
DOROTHY FIELDS

Melody by
JIMMY McHUGH

Don't Blame Me - 3 - 1

DON'T GET AROUND MUCH ANYMORE

Lyric by
BOB RUSSELL

Music by
DUKE ELLINGTON

Don't Get Around Much Anymore - 3 - 1

92

DREAMY

Words by
SYDNEY SHAW

Music by
ERROLL GARNER

Dreamy - 4 - 1

96

Dreamy - 4 - 3

EASY TO LOVE

Words and Music by
COLE PORTER

I know too well that I'm _____ just wast-ing pre-cious time in

think-ing such a thing could be, That you _____ could ev-er care for me,

Easy to Love - 3 - 1

Refrain (*slowly, with much expression*)

Easy to Love - 3 - 2

100

EUROPA
(Earth's Cry Heaven's Smile)

Music by
CARLOS SANTANA
and TOM COSTER

Europa - 5 - 1

104

EMBRACEABLE YOU

Music and Lyrics by
GEORGE GERSHWIN and IRA GERSHWIN

Embraceable You - 4 - 1

Embraceable You - 4 - 2

109

Embraceable You - 4 - 4

EMILY

Words by
JOHNNY MERCER

Music by
JOHNNY MANDEL

Moderately slow

Em - i - ly, Em - i - ly, Em - i - ly____ has the mur - mur - ing sound of May, ____ All sil - ver bells, cor - al shells, car - ou - sels____ and the laugh - ter of chil - dren at play say. Em - i - ly, Em - i - ly, Em - i - ly ____ and we fade to a

FALLING IN LOVE WITH LOVE

Words by
LORENZ HART

Music by
RICHARD RODGERS

Falling in Love With Love - 6 - 1

116

Falling in Love With Love - 6 - 6

FASCINATING RHYTHM

Music and Lyrics by
GEORGE GERSHWIN and IRA GERSHWIN

Fascinating Rhythm - 4 - 1

FINE AND DANDY

Words by
PAUL JAMES

Music by
KAY SWIFT

A FINE ROMANCE

Words by
DOROTHY FIELDS

Music by
JEROME KERN

won't ——— wres - tle! I might as well play bridge with my old maid
all ——— mor - als! I've ne - ver mussed the crease in your blue serge

aunts! ——— I have-n't got a chance, ——— this is a fine ro -
pants, ——— I ne - ver get the chance, ——— this is a fine ro -

- mance!

mf

A

128

just as hard to land as the 'Ile de France', I have-n't got a
ne - ver give the or - chids I send a glance, no, you like cac - tus

chance, this is a fine ro - mance!
plants, this is a fine ro -

A - mance! _____

A FOGGY DAY

Music and Lyrics by
GEORGE GERSHWIN
and IRA GERSHWIN

I was a strang-er in the cit-y.___ Out of town were the peo-ple I knew.

I had that feel-ing of self - pi-ty,___ What to do? What to do? What to do? The

A Foggy Day - 4 - 1

THE GENTLE RAIN

Music by
LUIZ BONFA

Words by
MATT DUBEY

The Gentle Rain - 2 - 1

rit. *a tempo* *rit.*

The Gentle Rain - 2 - 2

136

THE GIRL FROM IPANEMA
(Garôta De Ipanema)

Original Words by
VINICIUS DE MORAES
English Words by
NORMAN GIMBEL

Music by
ANTONIO CARLOS JOBIM

I LOVE YOU

Words and Music by
COLE PORTER

If a love song I could on-ly write,____ A song with words and

mu-sic di - vine____ I would ser - e - nade you ev - 'ry

night ____ Till you'd re - lent and con - sent to be mine ____ But a-

I Love You - 5 - 1

142

I Love You - 5 - 4

143

I Love You - 5 - 5

HAVE YOU MET MISS JONES

Words by
LORENZ HART

Music by
RICHARD RODGERS

Have You Met Miss Jones - 4 - 1

Have You Met Miss Jones - 4 - 4

HONEYSUCKLE ROSE

Words by
ANDY RAZAF

Music by
THOMAS "FATS" WALLER

Medium with a lift

Lyrics:

Ev-'ry hon-ey bee fills with jeal-ous-y when they see you out with me, I don't blame them, good-ness knows, _____ Hon-ey Suck-le Rose.

When you're pass-in' by flow-ers droop and sigh, and I know the rea-son why, You're much sweet-er, good-ness knows, _____

Honeysuckle Rose - 2 - 1

150

HOW HIGH THE MOON

Words by
NANCY HAMILTON

Music by
MORGAN LEWIS

How High the Moon - 2 - 1

HOW INSENSITIVE
(Insensatez)

Original Words by VINICIUS DE MORAES
English Words by NORMAN GIMBEL

Music by
ANTONIO CARLOS JOBIM

Moderately

How_____ in-sen-si-tive_____ I must_have seemed_____ when {he/she}
Now,_____ {he's/she's} gone a-way_____ and I'm a-lone_____ with the

told me that_ {he/she} loved____ me. How_____ un-moved_and cold
mem-'ry of_ {his/her} last____ look. Vague_____ and drawn_and sad,__

I must_have seemed.__ when {he/she} told me so__ sin-cere-ly.__
I see__ it still,____ all {his/her} heart-break in__ that last____ look.

I COULD WRITE A BOOK

Words by
LORENZ HART

Music by
RICHARD RODGERS

I Could Write a Book - 4 - 1

156

I Could Write a Book - 4 - 4

I GOT RHYTHM

Music and Lyrics by
GEORGE GERSHWIN
and IRA GERSHWIN

I Got Rhythm - 4 - 1

159

I Got Rhythm - 4 - 2

160

REFRAIN (with abandon)

I'LL REMEMBER APRIL

Words and Music by
DON RAYE, GENE DE PAUL
and PAT JOHNSTON

I'll Remember April - 3 - 1

164

I'll Remember April - 3 - 3

I'M BEGINNING TO SEE THE LIGHT

Words and Music by
DON GEORGE, JOHNNY HODGES,
DUKE ELLINGTON and HARRY JAMES

I'm Beginning to See the Light - 3 - 1

166

IN A SENTIMENTAL MOOD

By
DUKE ELLINGTON, IRVING MILLS
and MANNY KURTZ

In a Sentimental Mood - 2 - 2

IN YOUR OWN SWEET WAY

By
DAVE BRUBECK

1st Improvisation

171

In Your Own Sweet Way - 8 - 2

172

In Your Own Sweet Way - 8 - 3

2nd Improvisation

3rd Improvisation

176

In Your Own Sweet Way - 8 - 7

INVITATION

Music by
BRONISLAU KAPER

Invitation - 3 - 1

180

IT'S A RAGGY WALTZ

Words and Music by
DAVE BRUBECK

It's a raggy waltz, a raggy waltz, a raggy waltz
That I'm gonna dance with you.
Now that you've heard this very funny beat
Let me see if you can feel it in your feet.
Yeah, you've got it! Startin' to swing!
Just forget everything,
Raggy waltzin' with me.
It's not a waltz that's Viennese,
Johann Strauss 'twould never please.

It's a raggy waltz, a raggy waltz, a raggy waltz,
And no other dance will do.
And when the dance is through
You're gonna say,
"Never stop romancin', dancin' in this way
Makes me love you."
Out on the floor you'll be askin' for more
Raggy waltzin' with me.
Come dance with me.

It's a Raggy Waltz - 3 - 1

IT DON'T MEAN A THING

(If It Ain't Got That Swing)

Words by
IRVING MILLS

Music by
DUKE ELLINGTON

Lively

What good is mel-o-dy, what good is mus-ic, If it ain't pos-sess-in' some-thing sweet,___ It ain't the mel-o-dy, it ain't the mus-ic, There's some-thing else that makes the tune com-plete.

CHORUS

It don't mean a thing, if it ain't got that swing,___ (doo wah, doo wah,

It Don't Mean a Thing - 2 - 1

LAURA

Lyric by
JOHNNY MERCER

Music by
DAVID RAKSIN

Laura - 2 - 1

LI'L DARLIN'

By
NEAL HEFTI

Slow, smooth and sensuous

Li'l Darlin' - 2 - 1

LIMEHOUSE BLUES

Words by
DOUGLAS FURBER

Music by
PHILIP BRAHAM

Limehouse Blues - 4 - 1

192

Limehouse Blues - 4 - 3

Oh! Lime-house blues ___ I've the real Lime-house blues ___

Can't seem to shake ___ off those sad Chin-a blues ___

Rings on your fin - gers and tears for your crown ___ that is the sto-

- ry of old Chin-a-town. ___

last time only

LOVE IS HERE TO STAY

Music and Lyrics by
GEORGE GERSHWIN and IRA GERSHWIN

The more I read the pa-pers The less I com-pre-hend The

world and all its ca-pers And how it all will end. Noth-ing seems to be

Love Is Here to Stay - 4 - 1

Lyrics:
last-ing, But that is-n't our af-fair; We've got some-thing per-ma-nent, I mean in the way we care.

Refrain

It's ver-y clear Our love is here to stay; Not for a year But ev-er and a day.

LOVER MAN
(Oh, Where Can You Be?)

Words and Music by
JIMMY DAVIS, ROGER "RAM" RAMIREZ
and JIMMY SHERMAN

Lover Man - 4 - 1

Lover Man - 4 - 4

LUSH LIFE

Words and Music by
BILLY STRAYHORN

MAKIN' WHOOPEE!

Words by
GUS KAHN

Music by
WALTER DONALDSON

Makin' Whoopee! - 3 - 1

206

THE MAN I LOVE

Music and Lyrics by
GEORGE GERSHWIN and IRA GERSHWIN

Andantino semplice

When the mel-low moon be-gins to beam, Ev-'ry night I dream a lit-tle dream,

And of course Prince Charm-ing is the theme, The he for me. Al-

The Man I Love - 4 - 1

210

The Man I Love - 4 - 3

The Man I Love - 4 - 4

MEDITATION
(Meditacao)

Original Words by NEWTON MENDONCA
English Words by NORMAN GIMBEL

Music by
ANTONIO CARLOS JOBIM

Meditation - 3 - 1

Meditation - 3 - 2

214

Meditation - 3 - 3

MISS OTIS REGRETS
(She's Unable to Lunch Today)

Words and Music by
COLE PORTER

Miss Otis Regrets - 5 - 1

218

MISTY

Lyric by
JOHNNY BURKE

Music by
ERROLL GARNER

Misty - 3 - 1

222

MOOD INDIGO

Words and Music by
DUKE ELLINGTON, IRVING MILLS
and ALBANY BIGARD

224

Mood Indigo - 3 - 2

THE MORE I SEE YOU

Words by
MACK GORDON

Music by
HARRY WARREN

Andante

Each time I look at you is like the first time. ___ Each time you're

near me, ___ the thrill is new. ___ And there is noth-ing that I would-n't

do for ___ the rare de-light of ___ the sight of you. For, ___

The More I See You - 3 - 1

228

MY FUNNY VALENTINE

Words by
LORENZ HART

Music by
RICHARD RODGERS

My Funny Valentine - 5 - 1

230

232

My Funny Valentine - 5 - 4

MOONLIGHT IN VERMONT

Words by
JOHN BLACKBURN

Music by
KARL SUESSDORF

Moonlight in Vermont - 5 - 1

236

237

Moonlight in Vermont - 5 - 4

MY SHIP

Lyrics by
IRA GERSHWIN

Music by
KURT WEILL

My ship has sails that are made of silk, The decks are trimmed with

gold, And of jam and spice there's a par - a - dise in the

hold._____ My ship's a - glow with a

My Ship - 3 - 1

240

My Ship - 3 - 2

MY FOOLISH HEART

Words by
NED WASHINGTON

Music by
VICTOR YOUNG

Slowly and expressively

243

My Foolish Heart - 2 - 2

NIGHT AND DAY

French Version by
EMÉLIA RENAUD

Words and Music by
COLE PORTER

Night and Day - 4 - 1

246

Night and Day - 4 - 3

Night and Day - 4 - 4

OLD DEVIL MOON

Words by
E.Y. Harburg

Music by
BURTON LANE

ON A CLEAR DAY
(You Can See Forever)

Words by
ALAN JAY LERNER

Music by
BURTON LANE

On a Clear Day - 3 - 1

ONE NOTE SAMBA

Original Words by NEWTON MENDONCA
English Words by JON HENDRICKS

Music by
ANTONIO CARLOS JOBIM

Lightly, with movement

One Note Samba - 3 - 1

254

One Note Samba - 3 - 2

ON GREEN DOLPHIN STREET

Lyrics by
NED WASHINGTON

Music by
BRONISLAU KAPER

On Green Dolphin Street - 2 - 1

ONE O'CLOCK JUMP

By
COUNT BASIE

Moderate Bounce Tempo

One O'Clock Jump - 6 - 1

One O'Clock Jump - 6 - 2

260

PRELUDE TO A KISS

By
DUKE ELLINGTON, IRVING MILLS
and IRVING GORDON

Prelude to a Kiss - 3 - 1

266

QUIET NIGHTS OF QUIET STARS
(Corcovado)

English Words by
GENE LEES

Original Words and Music by
ANTONIO CARLOS JOBIM

Moderately slow

Quiet nights of quiet stars, quiet chords from my guitar floating on the silence that surrounds

Quiet Nights of Quiet Stars - 3 - 1

Quiet Nights of Quiet Stars - 3 - 3

'ROUND MIDNIGHT

Words by
BERNIE HANIGHEN

Music by
COOTIE WILLIAMS and THELONIOUS MONK

'Round Midnight - 6 - 1

272

'Round Midnight - 6 - 3

273

'Round Midnight - 6 - 4

274

SATIN DOLL

Words and Music by
JOHNNY MERCER, DUKE ELLINGTON
and BILLY STRAYHORN

Satin Doll - 2 - 1

SECRET LOVE

Words by
PAUL FRANCIS WEBSTER

Music by
SAMMY FAIN

SO NICE
(Summer Samba)

English Words by
NORMAN GIMBEL

Original Words and Music by
MARCOS VALLE and PAULO SERGIO VALLE

So Nice - 3 - 1

280

So Nice - 3 - 2

So Nice - 3 - 3

SKYLARK

Words by
JOHNNY MERCER

Music by
HOAGY CARMICHAEL

Moderately slow

Sky - lark, _____ have you an - y - thing to say to me?

Skylark - 4 - 1

SOLITUDE

Words and Music by
DUKE ELLINGTON, IRVING MILLS
and EDDIE DeLANGE

SOME OTHER TIME

Words by
BETTY COMDEN and ADOLPH GREEN

Music by
LEONARD BERNSTEIN

REFRAIN *Contemplatively*

290

SOPHISTICATED LADY

Words and Music by
DUKE ELLINGTON, IRVING MILLS
and MITCHELL PARISH

Sophisticated Lady - 3 - 1

SOMEONE TO WATCH OVER ME

French version by
EMÉLIA RENAUD

Music and Lyrics by
GEORGE GERSHWIN and IRA GERSHWIN

Scherzando

Moderato

There's a say-ing old Says that love is blind, Still we're of-ten told, "Seek and
Un pro-ver-be dit l'a-mour a - veu-glé, *On nous dit aus-si: "Cher-chez*

ye shall find." So I'm going to seek A cer-tain lad I've had in mind.
pour trou-ver." Je cher-che ce gail-lard qui m'est res-té dans l'i - dée,

Someone to Watch Over Me - 4 - 1

Someone to Watch Over Me - 4 - 2

REFRAIN

THE SONG IS YOU

Words by
OSCAR HAMMERSTEIN II

Music by
JEROME KERN

The Song Is You - 4 - 1

The Song Is You - 4 - 2

STAIRWAY TO THE STARS

Words by
MITCHELL PARISH

Music by
MATT MALNECK and
FRANK SIGNORELLI

Stairway to the Stars - 2 - 2

STAR DUST

Words by
MITCHELL PARISH
French Translation by
YVETTE BARUCH

Music by
HOAGY CARMICHAEL

Moderately

Some- times I won- der why I spend the lone- ly night
Sou - vent le si - lence de la nuit ré - pète ton nom

Dream- ing of a song? The mel- o- dy haunts my rev-er-ie, And I am once a- gain with
Comme un - e chan-son, Sa mél- o- die hante ma rêv- er-ie, Mon rêve me trans-porte dans tes

you,____ When our love was new, and each kiss an in-spir- a- tion,____
bras,____ Quand l'a - mour fût jeune, et chaque bai- ser in-spir- a- tion,

But that was long a- go: now my con-so-la- tion is in the star dust of a
Les ann- ées sont pass- ées et ma con-so- la- tion s'é- lève à l'é- toile d'une chan-

Star Dust - 2 - 1

STOMPIN' AT THE SAVOY

Lyric by
ANDY RAZAF

Music by
BENNY GOODMAN, CHICK WEBB
and EDGAR SAMPSON

Stompin' at the Savoy - 4 - 1

SUMMERTIME

By
GEORGE GERSHWIN,
DuBOSE and DOROTHY HEYWARD
and IRA GERSHWIN

Summertime - 4 - 1

Summertime - 4 - 2

morn - in'___ there's a noth - in' can harm you___

With Dad - dy an' Mam - my stand - in'

by.___

SWEET GEORGIA BROWN

Words and Music by
BEN BERNIE, MACEO PINKARD
and KENNETH CASEY

Sweet Georgia Brown - 5 - 1

SWEET LORRAINE

Words by
MITCHELL PARISH

Music by
CLIFF BURWELL

Sweet Lorraine - 3 - 1

Slow steady beat until end

TAKE FIVE

By
PAUL DESMOND

Take Five - 4 - 1

Take Five - 4 - 2

Take Five - 4 - 4

TEACH ME TONIGHT

Words by
SAMMY CAHN

Music by
GENE DePAUL

Teach Me Tonight - 2 - 2

THEY CAN'T TAKE THAT AWAY FROM ME

Music and Lyrics by
GEORGE GERSHWIN
and IRA GERSHWIN

Our ro-mance won't end on a sor-row-ful note, Though by to-mor-row you're

gone;___ The song is end-ed, but as the song-writ-er wrote, The

They Can't Take That Away From Me - 4 - 1

They Can't Take That Away From Me - 4 - 2

TIME AFTER TIME

Words by
SAMMY CAHN

Music by
JULE STYNE

Moderato

TIME AF-TER TIME I tell my-self that I'm so
Know what I know the pass-ing years will show you've

luck-y to be lov - ing you, _____ So
kept my love so

luck-y to be the one you run to see in the

Time After Time - 2 - 1

THE WAY YOU LOOK TONIGHT

Words by
DOROTHY FIELDS

Music by
JEROME KERN

The Way You Look Tonight - 4 - 1

The Way You Look Tonight - 4 - 2

unchanged

unchanged

WHAT'S NEW

Lyric by
JOHNNY BURKE

Music by
BOB HAGGART

What's New - 2 - 1

WATCH WHAT HAPPENS

English Lyrics by
NORMAN GIMBEL

Music by
MICHEL LEGRAND

342

Watch What Happens - 3 - 3

WILLOW WEEP FOR ME

Words and Music by
ANN RONELL

Willow Weep for Me - 5 - 1

344

Willow Weep for Me - 5 - 2

YOU MUST BELIEVE IN SPRING

Lyrics by
ALAN and MARILYN BERGMAN

Music by
MICHEL LEGRAND

YOU STEPPED OUT OF A DREAM

Lyric by
GUS KAHN

Music by
NACIO HERB BROWN

352

You Stepped Out of a Dream - 2 - 2

YOU'D BE SO NICE TO COME HOME TO

<div style="text-align: right;">Words and Music by
COLE PORTER</div>

Rather Slow with Feeling

You'd Be So Nice to Come Home To - 3 - 1

The *Ultimate* SHOWSTOPPERS *Series*

Movie

Piano/Vocal/Chords

More than 75 titles including: American Pie (from *The Next Best Thing*) • Chan the World (from *Phenomenon*) • Over the Rainbow (from *The Wizard of Oz* The Pink Panther • Tears in Heaven (from *Rush*) • There You'll Be (from *Pe Harbor*) • A View to a Kill • You Must Love Me (from *Evita*) and many more.

Television

Piano/Vocal/Chords

More than 115 TV titles including: Dharma and Greg • Every Beat of My Hear (from "As the World Turns") • The Pink Panther • The Power Puff Girls (En Theme) • Searchin' My Soul (from "Ally McBeal") • Sex and the City (Mai Title Theme) • Theme from "Chicago Hope" • Theme from "Magnum P.I." Theme from "The X-Files" • Walk with You (Theme from "Touched by a Angel") • Woke Up This Morning (from "The Sopranos") and many more.

Wedding

Piano/Vocal/Chords

More than 80 titles including: Evergreen (Love Theme from *A Star Is Born* • Forever I Do (The Wedding Song) • From This Moment On • I Do (Paul Brandt) • I Swear (All-4-One) • Let It Be Me (Je T' Appartiens) • Love Like Ours • This I Promise You • Tonight I Celebrate My Love • Two Hearts • The Vows Go Unbroken (Always True to You) • What a Difference You've Made in My Life • You're the Inspiration and many more.

Classic Rock

Piano/Vocal/Chords

Includes: Against the Wind • American Pie • American Woman • Cat's in the Cradle • Don't Let the Sun Go Down on Me • Evil Ways • Hey Nineteen • House at Pooh Corner • Layla • Lyin' Eyes • Nights in White Satin and many more.

Look for future additions to the *Ultimate* SHOWSTOPPERS *Series!*

Waller

Around the time Henry Mancini was born in the 1920s, another great composer was blending jazz with dramatic productions, this time not in Hollywood, but on Broadway. Thomas Wright "Fats" Waller was instrumental in bringing jazz out of the cabarets and clubs and into the theatre. A charismatic figure with an infectious sense of humor, Waller became a professional pianist at the age of 15, much against the objections of his clergyman father.

The New York-born pianist and composer became the toast of Broadway in the 1920s as his jazz songs were featured in the most popular plays. Beneath his humor and bravado, Waller was a wonderfully gifted jazz composer with an ability to be both lighthearted and moving in songs like "Ain't Misbehavin'" and "Honeysuckle Rose."

Like Brubeck, Mancini, and other great composers who followed him, Fats Waller proved in beautiful and convincing fashion that good jazz can be at home anywhere.

Jazz Trivia

• Fats Waller was the first jazz artist to incorporate the organ into his work.

• Ann Ronell, one of the few women in Tin Pan Alley, wrote the words and lyrics for the jazz classic "Willow Weep for Me." Later in her career, Ronell moved to writing film scores and received two Academy Award nominations.

• *The Jazz Singer,* starring Al Jolson, was the first "talkie" motion picture.

• Ironically, Duke Ellington's theme song, "Take the 'A' Train," wasn't written by Duke but by Billy Strayhorn, a pianist who joined the orchestra in 1939.

• George Gershwin's "I Got Rhythm" was introduced by Ethel Merman in *Girl Crazy* in 1930. Three years later, Gershwin arranged the song into a set of variations for piano and orchestra. His 32-bar structure of "I Got Rhythm" is said to be the second most often used harmonic progression in jazz improvisation, after the standard 12-bar blues progression.

high school students coming of age during this era, the music of Dave Brubeck and his fellow West Coast artists was their first exposure to jazz, starting them on a journey that would lead to an exploration of artists like Miles Davis, John Coltrane, Art Blakey, and—for the more daring souls—Ornette Coleman.

Mancini

While Dave Brubeck was bringing jazz to a wider audience with his West Coast sound, another young artist was popularizing a version of the musical genre in the world of film. His name was Henry Mancini. Born in the hard-edged mining town of West Aliquippa, Pennsylvania, Mancini was taught to play the flute by his father. As a youngster, Mancini took lessons from Max Adkins, a Pittsburgh concertmaster and jazz aficionado, who introduced the budding composer to Benny Goodman.

After graduating from high school, Mancini attended Carnegie Institute of Technology in Pittsburgh and, later, Juilliard in New York. While at Juilliard, he worked for bandleader

Vincent Lopez, enriching his understanding of jazz. A few years later, he drew on this experience when he was named the lead arranger for the 1954 film *The Glenn Miller Story*. This was followed two years later by a job as the arranger for *The Benny Goodman Story*.

Mancini's big break came when Blake Edwards asked him to write music for a new TV series, "Peter Gunn." Writing for an ensemble of 11 jazz musicians, Mancini created a dark, powerful composition that became one of the most popular TV theme songs of all time. "Music From Peter Gunn" reached No. 1 on the *Billboard* chart and remained there for ten weeks, introducing a new generation of fans to the jazz sound.

Teaming up with lyricist Johnny Mercer, Mancini created a series of smooth, sophisticated film and TV theme songs that drew heavily on his jazz background. The 1962 Academy Award-winning film song "The Days of Wine and Roses" epitomizes the urbane jazz-influenced style of the Mancini-Mercer team.

Brubeck

Like Ellington, pianist and composer Dave Brubeck painted his jazz landscape with broad and beautiful strokes, pushing his music to the limit with a breathtaking array of innovations. Brubeck learned the piano from his mother at the age of four and began playing the cello when he was nine. He led a 12-piece orchestra in college and, after serving overseas in the army, formed an experimental jazz workshop ensemble that recorded under the name The Dave Brubeck Octet.

As a composer, Brubeck has created a richly diverse body of work that includes ballets, a mass, cantatas, piano solos, and large-scale orchestral pieces. But he is best known throughout the world for his stunningly original jazz compositions. Many of his most innovative and celebrated songs have been recorded by The Dave Brubeck Quartet, with Brubeck on piano, Paul Desmond on alto saxophone, Joe Morello on drums, and Eugene Wright on double bass. Since its formation in the 1950s, The Dave Brubeck Quartet has become known and loved for

COUNT BASIE

pushing the envelope of jazz while still creating music with a popular touch. The group's experimentation with unusual time signatures in songs like the famous "Take Five" and "Blue Rondo à la Turk" established its worldwide reputation and opened new creative avenues for other jazz artists. A smash hit, "Take Five" earned the first Gold Record for a jazz LP and garnered Brubeck a place on the cover of *Time* magazine.

The popularity of The Dave Brubeck Quartet helped keep jazz in the popular mainstream during the 1950s, when the big band sound lost its once dominant influence on the pop charts. In fact, until its break-up in 1967, The Dave Brubeck Quartet served as an unofficial worldwide ambassador for jazz.

For much of the 1950s and 1960s, Brubeck, along with fellow artists Gerry Mulligan and Shorty Rogers, personified what came to be known as the West Coast jazz sound. A mellow version of cool jazz created by small improvisational groups, the West Coast sound featured soft, understated themes that blended elements of classical and jazz, more subtle vibratos (or no vibratos at all), and a more laid-back style of drumming. For many American college and

ELLA FITZGERALD

In the 1930s, Williams was one of the most celebrated jazz trumpeters in the world. He was a featured performer with many of America's leading bands, including Fletcher Henderson's orchestra, but he really hit his stride as a jazz musician during his 11 years with the orchestra of the great Duke Ellington.

During his tenure with the Duke, Williams expanded the emotional reach of his performances, covering a wider range of timbres with his mute technique. He also became a master of open horn playing, taking center stage during performances of songs like "Echoes of Harlem." Duke Ellington's evocative and plaintive masterpiece "Do Nothin' Till You Hear From Me" was known in its instrumental version as "Concerto for Cootie" in honor of the gifted trumpeter with a special flare for mute techniques.

Cootie Williams was only one of a legion of jazz artists who were influenced by the incomparable Edward Kennedy "Duke" Ellington. Although he was a brilliant pianist, Ellington's main instrument

LOUIS ARMSTRONG

was his orchestra. Few composers and arrangers in any musical genre were able to blend different instruments together as artfully as this dapper genius from Washington, D.C.

Exhibiting an other-worldly knack for harmonic invention, Ellington began experimenting with concepts like playing in several keys simultaneously in songs like "Azure" long before other musicians embraced these ideas. Underlying all of Ellington's music was a strong, confident, and cohesive rhythm section. It was a tribute to the talent of this great jazz composer that he gave every instrument in his orchestra a very distinct, individualistic personality, knowing he could blend them into seamless ensembles at a moment's notice whenever necessary.

Through his richly colored and subtle compositions, Ellington brought a new level of sophistication to jazz music while still paying proper respect to the improvisational tradition. His flair for combining different brass and woodwind instruments in new ways and his ability to weave symphonic devices into jazz compositions have given Ellington's music a dazzling originality that is still very much in evidence today in songs like "Mood Indigo" and "Sophisticated Lady."

CHARLIE PARKER

Ultimate JAZZ SHOWSTOPPERS

Introduction

Attempting to define jazz is akin to drawing a map of the human heart or taking a photograph of the wind. It's impossible to describe this endlessly captivating form of music in terms that are rigid or fixed. Like our hearts and the wind, jazz is forever changing, refusing to remain still or confine itself within convenient boundaries. Jazz always reinvents itself, not with each new generation, but with every performance.

For artist and audience alike, each jazz song is like opening a surprise package. The propulsive syncopated rhythms, creative improvisation, and deliberate distortions of pitch and timbre that characterize jazz transport us in unexpected ways, opening our minds and stretching our souls to embrace new visions.

Jazz has been through many transformations since it first appeared in the early twentieth century, when African-American musical traditions blended with European harmonies to create a distinctive new sound.

Ragtime, the forerunner of jazz, which grew out of the minstrel songs of America's South, became the country's most popular music by the close of the nineteenth century. Although jazz incorporated many elements of ragtime, particularly its syncopated melodies and themes, the new music offered something different and exciting—*improvisation*. Unlike ragtime, jazz music was not fully notated. Artists who performed the new music were expected to weave their own ideas into a composition when they played jazz. The spirit of improvisa-

DUKE ELLINGTON

tion has infused jazz with a unique dynamism that has run through the history of this brilliant musical genre, from New Orleans swing to orchestral jazz and big band, through bebop, free jazz, and jazz rock. But jazz is much more than improvisation alone; from its earliest days, it has also been a music of intricate techniques and subtle expressions.

Williams and Ellington

Both of these influences, free improvisation and the detailed technique, are evident in the music of trumpeter Cootie Williams. Born Charles Melvin Williams, Cootie became famous for his mastery of the plunger mute. His mute technique gave his trumpet playing a distinctive and very expressive growl-like sound on songs like "'Round Midnight."

CONTENTS

Ultimate JAZZ SHOWSTOPPERS

Project Managers: Carol Cuellar and Donna Salzburg
Art Design: Ken Rehm
Text By: Fucini Productions, Inc.
Photography: pages 4, 5, 6: Star File; all other photos: © DigitalVision Ltd.
Special thanks to David, Larry, Gail, Vincent, Mike, and Ken for their creative input